REMEMBERING VIETNAM AND OTHER THINGS

Dr. Lauren J. Ball

ISBN 978-1-953223-46-3 (paperback)

Copyright © 2020 by Dr. Lauren J. Ball

All rights reserved. No part of this publication may be reproduced, distributed, or transmitted in any form or by any means, including photocopying, recording, or other electronic or mechanical methods without the prior written permission of the publisher. For permission requests, solicit the publisher via the address below.

Rushmore Press LLC
1 800 460 9188
www.rushmorepress.com

Printed in the United States of America

I am a ninety-two-year-old veteran and retiree, having given twenty-four years and eight months to the United States Army. I have served in Germany just after WWII, Korea, Viet Nam, and many states. I have been promoted from private on through grade E-6 and then to chief warrant officer. I have seen this world go through many changes, most of them not so good.

Satan's work is never finished. He has changed this world from those who have served God to many who serve Satan. This hasn't happened overnight but through millennia and centuries, teaching false beliefs that have lasted down through the centuries, wreaking havoc on every country and every individual who has lived here, except Jesus Christ. Satan's work is to always satisfy a grudge that cannot be satisfied. His actions have caused pain, suffering, torture, and torment and even death to uncounted billions. God's plan is to let Satan test us through temptations, influences, and promptings, to see which path we would take—God's or Satan's.

The trials and tribulations we, as the human race, have gone and are going through is designed to strengthen us to see who we would rather serve, God or Satan. This earth life is the testing ground to see who we would rather follow.

What has this poetry got to do with God and Satan? As you read this work, you will see the effects of both God and Satan at work. Neither God's nor Satan's work is ever done, each will encourage us to follow one or the other. The choice, through our agency, will never change. These are the last days when God will separate the wheat from the tares. Let each of us decide now who we will follow!

This work may be hard for many to understand but continued analysis will help the reader grasp the meaning. I have used many different styles to help the reader comprehend this work. Good luck and God bless.

A CHRISTMAS GIFT

This poem is dedicated to our three-year-
old son who went back to the Father.
Written in Vietnam

        Adorned with lights
      And many tinseled hues,
    A small tree dies this night,
  And dying casts a glow
    Of loving tender light
      Upon a small
        Tousled
              Head of hair
                Where angels live,
        Where blue eyes
      Shine and dance,
    Where pure hearts flutter,
      And burst their bonds
        In the joy of love.
            Innocence and faith
        Rule here.
      Dragons live,
    Fairies dance and sing,
  And love,
With all its secrets
  Tells the pure in heart,
    About the great pumpkin
      To arise from his orange domain
        And cast an eerie giant shadow
          Upon a misty night.
      Elves sing their chant
    In forest glen
    And nature in her quiet way
  Bestows her gifts of love.
    Knights of old
      Are alive again.

                    The dragons fly
                 And the princess
               Is still the prize.
            Alice falls,
         Peter rabbit lives,
             And Billy beaver swims about.
                Christmas,
      Yes, Christmas is real too.
            Santa flies with reindeer.
                And Christ,
                    Who softly calls within
                       To love,
                             To live,
                       Whoever prompts the world,
                 That peace
              Goodwill towards men
      With hope, charity, with obedience
              To all His joyous laws
                    Will bring God's happiness
                          To all that ever lived within
                             A sweet young breast.
                    When hearts are wrung
                 And joyful teardrops
              Gleam and splash their joy
      Of all-consuming love
                 Within their soul.
                    They will know
                    That they are very close
                       To Him above,
                 Who gave them life
                 And breathed
              A sweetest breath
      Of purest love
                 Upon the face of all the world.
                    On each of us
                       He breathed His love.
                    For those whose hearts and minds
                 Are ever open wide,

For those whose selfish wants
Are cast aside,
For those who serve with love,
And joyful hearts
Of all mankind,
For those, whose greatest wish
Is for their fellow man,
For those whose searching arms,
Reach out and clasp our spinning world,
For those who cry at silly things,
Like favorite songs,
Like natures beauty scenes,
Like Johnny coming home.
For those who pray
With loves own dream,
In secret places kneel.
Yes, for those who love
The world this way,
A very special place is set,
Where love abounds,
Where cares and scars are swept away.
And on this special Christmas Eve,
A prayer for those, when love,
That all may find
This very special place
Where joy will never cease,
And may our watchful Father
Protect and keep us safe
From all the world's harm.

LONELINESS
Written in Vietnam

Loneliness casts
> An apprehensive shadow
> On the nights
>> When the steel winds blew.

> Justification was needed
>> To ease the dread
> Of imagination's seed.

>> Wildness encroached
> On unbridled thoughts
>> And seeks gratification
> Through unpremeditated action.

>> Thoughtless followers
Magnify escapism
>> Into flooded rivers of red,
And reap an undirected mass of chaos.

>> Histories ageless ribbon
Extends life's Cycle,
>> Where another chaotic mass
Of restless hate
>> Begat a destroyer's dream,
And emptied
>> The treasury dry.

Times measured thrust
Blasted reason's destiny
> Into limitless space,
And cried the past away.

      Changeless is gone,
But still yellows the future
      With cancer's malice.

Empty I walk the penniless present,
      And stumbling, grope my way
Past fallen stumps
      Of waving stubble.

The iron rod,
      Seems to melt,
Leaving my guilt-ridden search
      To fare alone.

Spires of loneliness
      Engulf the swirling vortex
Of my mind.
      The whirlwinds eye,
The blowing sand,
      Leaves a crimson wake
Of senseless pain.
      Somehow in loneliness,
I wonder and still survive.

WATCHES

I fear the dull day
    Even inconsistencies,
Breed inconsistences.
    Seen through a haze,
The green of the trees
    Melt into a crazy maze.

I wait for I know not what,
    And when it never comes,
I'm disappointed, and blame my wife
    And shout at my kids.

The end must be near,
    The rainbow has disappeared
From the mauve sky,
    And the rain
Is oil in the streets,
    With clouds of black smoke
Roiling in the sky.

    The ebon sand
Has crept into all the machinery.
    Where a street once was safe
We now find the horror of fear and
    Rivers of red flow easily
In towns now vacant and sad.
    Shattered panes of glass
And blank staring windows
    Tell tales of violent excesses.

My alma mater
    Has been changed
Into a hollow land of tears,
    Where echoes of terror are heard,

But chaos is not understood.
    Yet the plaintive cries
  Of the masses are no longer acknowledged.

My life which once had meaning
Has now been incarcerated
    In a bowl of black jello,
Which jiggles when I laugh
    My cry away.
Parkinson's law seems to have infiltrated
    Every aspect of my life.
Uncle's demands increase
    And each added encumbrance,
Sends its message
    In this abstract realm
        Of watches.

FREEDOM

Written in Vietnam

A humid land of heat and sun,
Where dust and rain and small things run.
A hell of tears and sweat and grime,
Where freedom's blood is shed in slime.

A thankless task that must be done
By brave young men who wield a gun
In swamps and mud mid jungles din,
Where rest or sleep can be a sin.

It's here we come to show the earth
Just what is meant by freedom's birth,
To let a Nation choose its fate
Before they're forced and it's too late.

Some say our lot is far too hard
That we from here be ever barred,
But they who speak in fear and dread
Have closed their minds to moral's stead.

They have not looked at years gone by,
When We sought help to do or die,
And from this aid our nation rose,
Where free men fight, their fates repose.

So, I for one will stay and fight,
To let Men choose from wrong or right,
And if by chance My life is lost
Let freedom's plaque be thus embossed.

WAR EXPOSED

Written in Vietnam

    Screaming and screaming,
    And running – must hide,
    Soft dark hole,
    Now I'm safe.
    I feel around, nothing to touch
Where? Why?
    Racking, stabbing, shooting pain.
    All is pain and mist.

    Pain fills my mind,
    With fear and angst, and light,
Far away.
Maybe I can reach it.
Must hurry – stay away. Just stay away.

The light, the light, so far away,
So very far, must go.
Rumbling, shuddering, violent earth,
Things falling.
Roaring sounds of hell where vapors rise.

The sky seems clear now,
Birds on the wing, red and blue.
White, pink flowers blend and die.
Leaving a stain on their beauty.

I'm falling, blackness comes.
Misty! Evil smelling! Turbulence!
I seem to slide into grey, then black.
A spot! A spot of changing light,
To pink then orange, then brown.

        I wriggle away and open wide,
          To engulf my mind.
Fear – run – speed away –
The voices – stop the voices.
The pain, screaming, streaming.
Shut up, shut up – can't think.

Must hurry to the light –
If I really run fast
Maybe I can make it.
So tired, so very tired.
Must sleep – must run – must sleep
Must go now——

WHY IS IT?

I made it and gave it a law,
Then placed it under glass.
      It grew lazy and self-indulgent,
      And ignored the law.

The food I gave it
Was rejected.
      And placed itself on the altar,
      Too many times.

Because of its darkness
I put a drop of water on it
      And started over.

Later, I painted it red
With its enemies,
      Which didn't do much good.
      Will they never learn?
      The time is very short now!

THE LAND OF THE NORTHERN LIGHTS

A tale is told when the nights are cold
And the fire is sinking low
Where the shadows dance and seem to enhance
The mood of the shivering blow.

Of a time long past when the die was cast
And fate was given its head
To use its might for a single night
On those who were easily led.

The lure of gold had brought the bold
To search this virgin land,
To wreck in haste and leave in waste,
For nature's healing hand.

It was here we felt that hands were dealt
By those who reigned above
To men like me who wouldn't flee
This State we came to love.

We watched at night as the northern lights
Would shimmer and dance and change
The cold north sky to a colorful lie,
Making ghosts of the mountain range.

Many men came for a chance at fame,
And others to rob and plunder.
Some were bold but none I'm told
Like him who came like thunder.

His name was Paul, he was kinda small,
But his fists were made of steel,
And many a man had failed to stand
Under the reign of his fist and heel.

He'd walked this land from Ketchikan
To the cold of north Point Barrow
And matched his wits with nature's fits,
Yet lived to see tomorrow.

He'd walked on ice that was there to entice,
The unwary to an early grave,
For the glacier's way is a subtle play
With death as the wanton slave.

It started one day across the bay
In an old log cabin we'd made.
It was forty below and beginnin' to snow
And the sun was startin' to fade.

When in came a man who said he was Stan,
He was six feet eight or so.
Said he'd came when he'd heard Paul's name
From the lips of one we know.

You could tell by his face he'd been in a race
With the wind and the snow and the cold
And through his eyes you could feel the cries
Of a soul that was tortured and old.

Every one of us had cause to discuss
The deeds of this devil Stan,
For he lived to kill the spirit and will
Of those who called his hand.

We heard him swear and say he'd tear
The heart from Paul's cowardly breast
If he was man enough and made of the stuff
To stand and meet the test.

You could almost see the courage flee
From every man in there
Except for Paul who wouldn't stall
The one's surly dare.

We felt the breath and stench of death
As they stood there glaring out
Of eyes of hate and with unwavering fate,
The cause for little doubt.

Now Stan moved first and his eager thirst
Carried him half across the floor
But there he was fell by a fist from hell
And hurled through the oaken door.

The cabin shook as his dazed look
Gave way to a bellow of rage.
He was quick to his feet for there he must meet
The tiger burst out of his cage.

The walls were strong, and you think me wrong,
But they stood for only a while,
Then like it was loaded the cabin exploded,
And the fight was on in style.

Bid brownies fight from dusk 'til light,
They gnash an' tear and rend,
But I've never seen such a bloody scene
As they fought to eternity's end.

Far into the night we could hear them fight
Like beasts from out of the past
But slowly the sound from those who were bound
Diminished and ebbed to the last.

When the silence came it wasn't the same
As that which had long been there
For the cries of the doomed had somehow bloomed,
On the eerie midnight air.

From the pitch-black night came an eerie sight
Of a ghostly apparition,
Rising up from the ground eternity bound
On the wings of superstition.

Their eyes on fire with the only desire
To destroy with lust and hate,
Condemned forever for they could not sever
The struggle that ended their fate.

There are those who say at the end of the day
When the northern lights are high,
They can sometimes see the ghostly sea
Where eternity draws nigh.

Where the ghostly fight in the luminous light
Rages on thru eternal mists.
You can hear their wail as they onward sail
And see their crashing fists.

Now don't look long for only the strong
Can endure this terrible sight.
Then the call may come and you be the one
That is damned to share their plight.

LIFE

After many eons passed
And I had finished my trial
My Father called me to His side
And said I must go earth-side for a while.

To learn of many wondrous things.
To prepare me for my place
Where I can truly prove myself
With intelligence and grace.

The faith and love he has for me,
And I for Him so great
For helping me to have my chance
To choose from love or hate.

And now that I am here on earth
My memories left behind,
Except for traces here and there
Which I nurture with my mind.

I contemplate the many games
That life is giving me
To solve, to play, to love, and bless,
The reasons for man to be.

I'll cherish life and strive to choose
The best that life can give
To gain from every thought
And action that I live.

I'll embrace the trials that cause me pain
And love this life so dear.
I will serve and give my all
To the children I hold so near.

Man may scoff at God and say
That he is ever dead,
And yet without His laws and love
Man's future is never said.

For the nearer man can be to God
The less there is a need
To control the myriad acts of men
Who suppress His wondrous seed.

The songs of life, most cherished songs,
Whose tunes have made man free
And entices me to new frontiers
That always encourage me.

Where life's progressions never end
And on, whose wings I'll fly,
To greater knowledge, a greater life,
With those who live on high.

And if I've loved this life I've lived
And lived this life I love,
Fulfilled, obeyed, the cherished laws
Of Him who rules above,

My mate and I will ever go
Together hand in hand
Thru eternal Mists of life and time
With God we'll make our stand.

For God's we'll be and answer to
Our own great God of fame
Creating worlds without end
To Glorify His name.

So, on and on progression goes,
A chance for all to gain,
To learn and live the mighty laws,
And gain a place with God to reign.

(Be ye therefore perfect, even as your Father,
which is in heaven is perfect. Matt. 5-48)

EMPATHY

Written in Vietnam

A grizzled mutt of a dog
Ambled his time worn hide
Over the same trail as I
That yellow monotonous day.

Scarred and matted
From life's endless battles,
Yet with a proud stance and lordly gait,
He approached unflinchingly.

Being aware of the trail myself,
I stopped for a moment to stare.
He stopped too,
And with shaggy head lifted,
Being curious as I.

Our eyes met and we empathized
For just a moment or two.
Then kind of sorrowfully and nostalgically,
We passed and went our way.

EXPANSIONS IN ABSTRACT IMAGERY

A nebulous void
      of wailing cosmic dust
            and silent streaming light
      where spiraling vapor mists
spawn ethereal life.

Pulsate rays of rainbow hues
      like hot blown glass
melt and waft away
      to gray and shadow shades.

Music chimes of pure esthetic sound
         haunt and probe
      these shatter worlds,
which sooths the clear enticing
      wrap-around tones
that ebb and throb their life away.

Speeds in breathless blur
      transcend this endless time
      on wings of white-hot fire
      that whips my arrow face
in passing thru beyond.

Salt-spray tears
      have dropped their splash
         and made the slanting rain,
      the thunderclap,
the lightening split its jagged streak
      toward an unknown end.

Thru a phase of vast new space
        the solar whirlwind spins
its half-formed life
        on each throbbing orb.
Eons soar the stars away
        Where time will ever cast
                its silver webs of light,
                      its prism rays,
                thru blackest voids of night
        to strike an image thought.

Wisps of acrid fumes
        Where their cosmic wastes,
        their billowing orange hot clouds
        from hell's deep gurgling pit,
leaving stifling after tastes
        of acids' bitter strife.

Gothic like the multicolored spires
        Of translucent crystal ice,
                catches and reflects
        the exquisite spray
of flowered beams,
        of dancing lights,
                on marbled walls,
in quiet blue-green pools
        of living liquid life.

FUTILITY IN RETROSPECT

The fireplace flames
Dance their orange light
Across the cobwebs of my mind
And penetrate their warmth
Thru the murky labyrinths
Of forbidden anxieties.

Sparks flare their radiance
Into the hollow cold
Of remembrance
And melt my icicle heart
Into a warm smile of forgiving.

The living embers
Breathe their heat
Into the well of my heart
And strengthens
the soft chair of my desire.

The curling smoke lifts my dauntless spirit
And forms an echo image
Thru the twilight mists
Of many happy hours.

Visions wrap their swirling tendrils
Around the fingers of my mind,
And again, renew the lost and forgotten
Hopes, of a treasured youth.

The whip-crack of splitting embers
Forge an explosive desire
To again regain a foothold
In the cliff-like steps of life.

But as I watch the fading flames,
The shrinking embers,
My commitment wavers,
And then like the fire, wastes into ashes,
again, the coldness of despair creeps in;
At last the winter snows beckon.

LADY LUCK

Adorned with jewels and raiment fine,
All silk and wispy feather light,
Touched by gold and thinly veiled,
A luring, ever magic sight,
Enticing me to fortunes gain.

A calling, prodding, smiling,
Tempting, shining, winking eye,
She clasped my hand,
Her lovely charms beguiling,
Leading, guiding, protecting my cast,
To win and win again,
Emotions rise and burst their bonds,
I soar and chuckle, and life is vain,
Meaningless, for I am perched on upon a cloud.

The world is mine, and mine alone,
For lady luck has touched my lips,
Her charms are mine to use and tone,
The dice to make them pay,
My will, my fortunes grow,
An ever faster beating heart,
A glistening brow.

I know that I must place my fortune gained
Upon that dark enchanted number,
Which lady luck has whispered soft
That all but one this time will slumber.
Thirteen is what I name,
That superstitious dark and loathsome pyre,
Upon whose all-consuming flame,
Does rest the fate of all who aspire
To get their gain from worldly stores,
Without their normal efforts spent,

The spinning wheel, and all is hush,
Emotions rise, desire sent,
To help control the dizzy wheel,
To make it stop and speak their will.

But deep within my burning breast,
I know that I must win
For still she sits,
this Lady Luck,
With ease upon my knees,
Her outstretched hand,
still guiding, gentle as a breeze,
To slow the wheel yet marking time.

She laughs and watches every face,
And not a breath is heard or spent,
For all is still, the quiet, deep.
The turning stops, the wheel has rent,
Her verdict on the silent scene.
With eyes I see, not willing to believe,
My fortune swept away and gone.

And Lady Luck, with beauty to deceive,
With riant, stifling laughter,
Took her leave, emotions sated,
But for just awhile,
And then a great new conquest rated
Her smiling beguiling charms.

And with her stifled laughter mocking,
An echo in my hollow mind,
I stopped myself from reeling, rocking,
Looking deep within my tortured heart,
I searched and knew the bitter truth
That some are born to win their part
And others just to lose their souls
Controlled by all the lovely charms
Of sweet beguiling Lady Luck.

WE ARE ALL HERE AS CHILDREN OF GOD

WE ARE HERE TO SEEK AND CHERISH ALL THAT IS RIGHTEOUS,
BEAUTIFUL, UPLIFTING, AND SPIRITUALLY ENLIGHTENING
AND TO IDENTIFY, REJECT, AND EXPUNGE
ALL THAT IS EVIL, UGLY, CORRUPTING, PLUS THAT WHICH IS
PHYSICALLY, MENTALLY, AND SPIRITUALLY DEGRADING.

WE ARE MUCH MORE THAN FORM.
WE ARE MAGNIFICENT, REMARKABLE,
SPLENDID, LOVING, ETERNAL, INTELLIGENCES
UNFETERED, UNLIMITED, AND UNSTOPPABLE.

WE ARE THE PERFECT EXPRESSION OF GOD'S LOVE,
THEREFORE, WE ARE PERFECT IN HIS LOVE.
WE ARE HERE TO EXPRESS AND MAGNIFY OUR LOVE FOR GOD
BY EXTENDING IT UNCONDITIONALLY
BACK TO HIM AND TO EVERYONE.
OUR ABILITY TO EXPRESS IT DEPENDS
ON HOW MUCH OF IT WE HAVE ACCEPTED FROM HIM
AND HOW WELL AND HOW OFTEN WE EXTEND IT TO OTHERS.

WE ARE HERE TO LEARN HOW TO RETURN TO GOD'S PRESENCE
THROUGH SCRIPTURE STUDY, OBEDIENCE, REVELATION,
INSPIRATION, GUIDANCE, AND PRAYER.
OTHER THAN BEING LOVE,
WE SHOULD NEVER DEFINE OURSELVES, FOR IN SO DOING,
WE SET BOUNDARIES AND LIMITATIONS
ON WHAT WE ARE AND WHAT WE CAN BECOME AND ACHIEVE.

WE ARE HERE TO DEVELOP FAITH, COMPASSION,
UNDERSTANDING, PATIENCE,
KINDNESS, HUMILITY, AND ALL OTHER RIGHTEOUS TRAITS
TO ACCEPT OURSELVES AND EVERYONE
FOR WHO AND WHAT WE TRULY ARE, CHILDREN OF GOD.

WE ARE HERE TO EXPERIENCE LIFE, GROW SPIRITUALLY, GAIN
KNOWLEDGE, WISDOM, INTELLIGENCE,
AND TO CREATE OURSELVES AS WE WANT TO BE,
GOOD, EVIL, OR UNCARING.
WITH GOD'S HELP IT WILL BE GOOD.

WE ARE HERE TO HELP RAISE THE LEVEL OF SPIRITUAL GROWTH
OF OUR CONSCIOUSNESS AND SPIRITUALITY
THROUGH KINDNESS, SERVICE, AND LOVE.
WE ARE HERE TO FORGIVE, REPENT, SEEK FORGIVENESS,
AND IN RIGHTEOUSNESS, ONLY PASS
JUDGMENT ON ACTIONS, NOT PEOPLE.
ALSO, WE ARE HERE TO LEARN HOW TO PERFECT
AND CONTROL OUR THOUGHTS, EMOTIONS, AND ACTIONS
AND TO PURIFY OURSELVES OF ALL EVIL
AND SPIRITUAL UNCLEANNESS,
WHICH BRINGS US ALL CLOSER TO GOD.

WE ARE HERE TO ACCEPT AND TREASURE ALL ORDINANCES
PERTAINING TO OUR SALVATION AND EXALTATION
AND TO HELP OTHERS IN THEIR QUEST TO DO THE SAME.

WE ARE ALSO HERE TO EXAMINE OUR BELIEFS
AND DETERMINE WHICH ARE TRUE AND WHICH ARE FALSE
AND SELECT THE TRUE ONES TO LIVE BY AND EXPAND,
ALSO TO EXPUNGE THOSE THAT ARE NOT TRUE.

FINALLY, I AM HERE TO IDENTIFY, OVERCOME, CONQUER,
AND RISE ABOVE ALL ADVERSITIES, ILLNESSES,
SATANICAL TEMPTATIONS AND PROMPTINGS,
ALL UNRIGHTEOUS TRAITS, CHARACTERISTICS,
MALADIES, LIMITATIONS, AND DIFFICULTIES
ALL WITH THE HELP OF
GOD, JESUS CHRIST, AND THE HOLY GHOST.

CHANGING

IF WE LIKE OURSELVES THE WAY WE ARE
AND WE KNOW WE'RE NOT PERFECT
BUT WE'RE NOT WILLING TO CHANGE
WE HAVE FOUND OUR NICHE IN ETERNITY...

IF WE DON'T LIKE OURSELVES
THE WAY WE ARE,
AND WE KNOW WE MUST CHANGE.
WE WILL STRIVE TO DO OUR UTMOST,
TO BECOME MORE LIKE GOD.
OUR NICHE, THEN, IS CHANGEABLE,
AND WE CAN BECOME
WHATEVER WE ARE WILLING TO BECOME.
OUR WILLINGNESS TO CHANGE
DETERMINES OUR PROGRESS
IN ETERNITY WITH GOD.

ONE OF THE MOST DIFFICULT ENDEAVORS
WE CHILDREN OF GOD HAVE
ON THIS EARTH IS TO BE WILLING AND ABLE
TO LOOK INWARD AND IDENTIFY THE AREAS OR TRAITS
THAT NEED SPIRITUAL HELP TO REFINE AND PERFFECT.
IF WE RECOGNIZE THAT WE DON'T HAVE THE ABILITY TO CHANGE,
WE NEED TO CALL ON HEAVENLY FATHER
FOR THAT ABILITY.
IF WE HAVE THE WILLINGNESS AND THE ABILITY
AND THEN DON'T ACT
OR WE DON'T HAVE THE KNOWLEDGE
OR WISDOM TO ACCOMPLISH IT,
WE DEFINITELY NEED TO CALL ON HEAVENLY FATHER
FOR HIS HELP, AND THEN IF WE DON'T ACT
OUR NICHE IS SET FOR ETERNITY.

WEALTH

WEALTH SHOULD NEVER BE MEASURED
BY OUR ACCUMULATION OF PHYSICAL POSSESSIONS
NOR BY THE PRESSURED OBEDIENCE
TO GOD'S LAWS AND COMMANDMENTS,
BUT BY HAPPY, UNPRESSURED OBEDIENCE AND LOVE
FOR GOD AND THE MEANING BEHIND
THE LAWS AND COMMANDMENTS...

DEATH

DEATH IS A RELEASE FROM THE BONDAGE OF SINNING,
AND THE DEGRADATION OF PAIN AND SUFFERING,
AND THE LIMITATIONS OF MORTAL LIFE.
TO MAKE THIS TRANSITION A HAPPY EXPERIENCE,
DO SO IN A STATE OF COMPLETE REPENTANCE
AND OBEDIENCE.

LOVE AFFIRMATION

HEAVENLY FATHER, PLEASE HELP ME TO EMBRACE
AND ACTIVATE MY FAITH TO ADAPT,
MAGNIFY, AND EXPAND THE FOLLOWING UNIFYING TRAITS:
LOVE, HOPE, AND CHARITY, TO HELP ME PERFECT MY LIFE.
I AM NOW EXTREMELY DETERMINED TO HONOR AND OBEY
THIS ESSENTIAL AFFIRMATION, WHICH WILL PENETRATE
TO THE VERY DEPTHS OF MY MIND, BODY, AND SPIRIT.
IN THE HOLY NAME OF JESUS CHRIST, AMEN.

VEXATION

Charred dolls
aren't real anymore
that all happened
before the tight tent nights
seemed to solve the clinging mystery,
but evolution set in and strained
the angry rebellion.

Sadness floats o'er my hanging head
and stillness sinks my aching heart.
The dead would wail, but for the birth,
New poignancy built on the spring rose
With thorns dulled by time.

Exquisite adventures into many untaught realms
Flood our eager doors.
Many paths we tread in different space times,
Chimes we hear from different calendars.
Just a touch here and there
And we know the water runs deep,
And sunken clocks will bear pain no more.

A new dawn has broken
And though we're forced to ride
The ghost shadows of parental affliction,
For a space, we can still smile
And bear the load with light.

Greetings will still come and the base will shift,
But the arrow's shaft our joy
As each birth regains its place.

Nostalgically I wait as my pen grows tired,
And I yearn for its return.
The rose I'll stretch and twist the pansy head,
Crush the fern and tread the flower bed.
When next our eyes are pierced,
Then long the race will flutter my heart,
And it is better on my part if I win.

PARI PASSU

O' glittering earth,
Whose mighty oceans heave,
And spawn life's flowing chains,
where endless mountains
stretch their glistening snow-white-arms
to search for heaven's rest.

O' shivering earth,
Whose frozen fingers stab
And pierce the warm blood hearts,
Where icy tendrils search ever south
To form a changing world.

O' wavering earth,
Whose fickle lands
Obtrude, dissolve,
Man's clutching long-held dreams.

O' shimmering earth,
where iridescent
dancing northern lights,
engulf man's beauty seeking heart
and fill it over full.

O' hideous earth,
Whose bloody streamlets flow
On ravaged war-torn lands,
where hate and greed are loosed
to reign and rule
man's ever receptive mind.

O' bitter earth,
where seeds of strife are sown
and bonds our grasping roots,
which seeks an end to man's prolific life.

O' joyous earth,
Where gentle love abounds
In innocent array
Among the open hearts
who search
for Christ's lost stars.

TRUTH

In Heaven I sat and placed my law.
Thru flood, smoke, and fire,
I spoke my word,
Created breath and death
For all to hear.

In this gurgling pit's red maw,
I've planted my Keys,
Which are well hidden
In words, in leaves, and rocks,
And in natures living cells
Those who really seek, will find.

I never push to break the balance bond
Between good and evil.
Six times I've watched
And sobbed My twisting heart
All to no avail.
Only My searchers have done their part.
I've thrust my head above this swirling pond,
And now the time to reap
Is near at hand.
The keys at last have been unveiled
Just as prophesy has planned.

At last I've cast My searcher's net
And claim My treasured prize.
From out the ground
My last word cries,
Come to me and we will be
One with God for eternity.

WHEN THE END COMES

The river's edge beckons onward to the flow
And spellbind the receptive into immobility.
The dust threatens to engulf its purveyors,
But when my God speaks it will create sparks,
Which gather round about.

The sting of the whip singing its song
Triumphs only over the fearful
Who accepts defeat as escapism.

The white lily floating on its embryonic pad
Is threatened beyond redemption
By the black inundation of creeping excesses.

The stark outline of a smoking silhouette
Attests to the macabre attitude
Of the swarming stifling insects.

And yet, the quiet can be heard
Above the silence.
The spring leaves can yet be heard above the jets.
The still soft sun in its coldness,
Warms the throbbing heart
As it purges its way to the sea.
When the end comes,
Where will we be?

WILL WE EVER LEARN?

From where I sat, I placed my law.
Thru smoke and fire
I spoke my word,
Created breath and death
For all who heard.

In this gurgling pit's red maw,
The keys I've planted
And hidden well,
In words, in leaves,
In nature's living cell.

I ever push to break the balance bond.
Six times I've watched
And cried My twisted heart.
Only My searchers
Have done their part.

I thrust my head above this swirling pond,
And now the time to reap
Is near at hand.
The keys at last unveiled,
Just as Prophets have planned.

At last I cast My searcher's net
And claim
My treasured prize.
From out the ground
My last word cries,
Which keys are love, and truth,
That never dies.

THE FOURTEENTH ROSE

Softly, touched our hands and joined,
Our new-found pain,
Entwined their mesh of bright new love
Around our throb-worn hearts,
Thus. Enslaved, our vows were made
On cactus, rock, and flame.

Love drops we planted
In our rose garden of fertility,
And reaped the matchless, the futile, the rebellious,
And still our flowers bloom.

Our twisted pride has often built a wall,
To crush, to stall,
But the roses have caused its fall.

Our roses of anguish, fear, love, patience, and pain,
Fill our cups with hot turgid love.
The reapers moans, absolve and dissolve
Our years of retreating strife
And cast their beams upon the iron rod
Where slippages are fraught
With the searchers knife.

The white rose years have come to cleanse,
Renew our hope and cast its rays
On our sturdy base,
Still built on cactus, rock, and flames.

TOMORROW I'LL AWAKEN
Written in Vietnam

A pinch of purple
Splashed its red impression
Across an otherwise
Drab landscape,
And swirled my mind.

Swollen and brutish
I lay by the stump
As the vermin from hell
Ate my entrails
And the blue-black buzzards
Danced at my wake.

I watched for a time
As the red spring rose
Softened my soul
On its velvet touch,
But it wafted away on the wings
Of the summer heat
And dried its petals on my heart.

Lost and wanting
I searched the desolation
For a caring moment, for a smile
Unapathetic in its design,
And found in the desolation
A black drop of red.

Then pain issued a statement of protest
As it carved its sting
Across the roads to my mind.
I watched and wept

As the clouds of sorrow
Crept through the face of my Father.
The pain of his land
Was now felt on the empty streets.
The toads now live where I once lived,
And on the trail once trod,
A golden goat laughs hideously
And where I once lay
I can now count the thorns.

I tried again but fled in anguish.
He knew I had been here
Once again – once before.
He fled before I arrived,
But he still knew.

Now I try to gain solace
As my cold hard steps echo
In the darkness
But the ranting of the past
Ever watches,
Like a sleepless sentry
Watching the crowds rush in.

My Mother
Still descends
Like some dark omen,
And garnishes my remembrance
Of many unthoughtful incidents.
Still she serves a magnificent need,
Or the sun would stay down.

Thickness impinges its desires
On the edge of my thoughts.
The lunatic fringe attempts
To steal my impregnated bowels—
And would, but I'm not alone.

Tomorrow I'll awaken, and the streams
Will rush their clear waters again.
The sun will dance through the green forests.
The lofty mountains will be white.
The sky will be blue,
I will hear the wind again,
and the robin will sing.

I can thank my Father without fear,
And he will stay near.
I'll go to the rainbow when I like.
I'll help my sons and daughters,
And the truth will live in every book.
The blades of grass will wave to me.
Tomorrow I'll awaken.

THE PAIN OF YOU

When love binds my mind
And ties my open heart
With unyielding bonds
That twist my hazy joy,
I sing with my breathless find.
I wave my heady thoughts away
And sway to the rhythm
Of my happy heart.
Even when apart, the chimes rhyme
With our play.
Weekends I gain in the pain
of you and etch our joy
In the soft clay of existence
When exchanging our gifts
Of invisible force before the train.
We often bargain for a compromise
And each in our own way
Pays for the promises we make.
In tears we oft' renew our pact
And cling to our fruitful ties.
The boundless environs
Of our thoughts enmesh our love
In a bright net of hope,
And as the golden leaves fall
On the autumn bed of our fulfilment,
The pain of our love
Will grow,
As the winter snows beckon.

WHERE ANGELS DWELL

With Angels I wept when she went away,
I emptied my heart
And my soul that day.
I share with her now though she be gone
The flowers she touched,
Her favorite song.

I walk with her beside me still,
On the shaded paths we once knew well.
Still my spirits are lifted high
By a long remembered "You're my Guy"

The quiet green spring pond
Mirrors my sorrow, my tears
But a knowledge of angels
Has quieted my fears
And our sharing of love
Can never end;
Some-how where angels dwell
We'll join together again.

WIND WILLOW

Swaying
    with the strange wind willow,
        Caressing her softness
On the eyes of my mind,
        Feeling with her gentle touch,
    A sharing one with another
        An instant in time.

Singing
    With the wildlife stream
        Building a dreamer's dream
    Where-in our creations live
        And to each, a joy, a love,
    With fulfillment give.

Stillness
    Seeks entry into our open hearts
        Bringing new strength
    As our love imparts.
        And ever as we touch,
    And hold,
        We silence
    The outside cold.

ON THE TRAIL WITH YOU

The soft blue sky bridged the gap
Between you and I,
And sitting
On the cool night air,
My heart holding you there,
Wept.

With joy it wept
And into it you crept,
Leaving behind a trail of softness,
Into which my mind has often slept.

The cradle of my desire,
With sweetness
tempts not my ire.
The ladle you raise
To my proffered lips
Is seen through a misty haze,
And my eyes will never tire.

The open cactus-flower
Offers its treasures,
And the strange saguaro
Looms large in the shade,
But the quiet green blade
Stores its pleasures for you and I.

The sunset of our lives
Shall not diminish
The winters' snow,
Nor quell the range
Of the searching skies
In the twilight of my life.

The flowing waters
From the mountains ice
Entice like sparkling eyes
Into whose depths I swim,
And dim though my sight may be
I see the harvest you gave unselfishly
Is still ours, in the blue green sea.

THE LONG THIN LINE

Susceptible in my own way
        To the darkling thrusts,
        And the nebulous meanderings
        Of chaotic ghosts,
    My boasts go unheard
        In the dire susceptible casualty
        And in my own way
        Into the arms
        Of the confused.

Enlightened in my own way,
    I still take refuge
    In the caves of forgetfulness,
And laugh to tunes
    The idlers play.
With open eyes
    I sleep with the rest of the blind.

With blue seeds planted
    On the baron rocks,
    And in the nearby crevasses,
        I trustingly watch
        For signs of life,
    But the chill wind rushes in
        And bids me leave,
        So, I sigh again
        And walk away.

I climbed a mountain once,
    And the only one that followed
    Was the chaotic Ghost.
I paused on a lifeless, lonely plateau
    And spoke of strange new things,
    Of bending thoughts,

        On gossamer wings.
So, changed I flowed
        Over the searchers path
        Where the chasm loomed.

Ninety-two clocks
        Mock the cardioidal mire,
        In which a half-gown ghost
        In a celluloid cell,
            Broke the staff,
        On the edge of the murky unknown
        At the bottom of a broken well,
            Where eternities dwell.

SURVIVOR

The plains of Tarza
like a diamond's fire
awoke in me a nomadic desire—
a restless, dreamer's urge
to purge my sardonic presence
in my long-held past.

Awakened and armed with vibrating sinew
And stark awareness
Of gravity smoldering below
I felt the flow of silent, sinking thought,
Attesting to my desire to flee the past.

Walking with Him beside me
Is not always easy, so, I sing a lot,
And let the snow-white cold
Vex my ire into a burning fire,
Which balm cannot diminish
Or quell my desire.

Sinking behind me,
Like a demonic artist gone wild,
Made a fading splash of a violent sun,
Making fun of the red-hot havoc
He left behind.

Ignoring the steps beside me
I stare straight ahead,
And build my bed with paper tales,
While the gales tear
At the frail threads I created,
Which seems, now to bleed its necessity away.

Just hanging around, like a long-lost clown,
I vowed to change my lust,
Or bust my part of life's wheel
Into slowly moving spokes,
But the joke's on me
If I flee this rotating reel.

In the far distance looms the white-hot peak,
I seek to sooth my frozen limbs.
Yet the silver threads I've woven
Have proven their strength
And my undoing.

I call in vain for Him to again walk beside me
But the sloping distance
Is far too great for Him to hear,
And my simmering fate
Is far too late,
As I stand here alone.

Intensified in a thick, murky solution,
The clear stain of a glass-like existence
Lies hidden and unbidden to emerge
Until its slag-like glaze
Is shattered, to release
In a blaze of glory
The silence of pure power.

Grasping at thin gold threads
While lying in beds of ego straw,
I gnaw at simple, multiple bonds
of the forging years
that only tears can wash away.

I pray now for the mocking past,
To catch each flying truth,
As I pause for the wind of a pure fresh breath.
And I listen now
For the quiet sure steps beside me.

LONG RANGE PATROL

Written in Vietnam

I was kinda keyed up that night,
Maybe it was because this was my first night to be alone.
Well, I wasn't really alone,
There were eleven of us,
But we were spread out
Alongside the trail.
So, we couldn't be so easily seen.
The stars shouted loud-like.
And you wished, the wind would be still,
So you could hear better.
I could see up the trail quite way
In the pale moonlight.
Everything seemed spooky,
And I wished I was about anywhere but here.
Then, jauntily as you please,
This Charley comes down the trail sort of humming.
I felt my guts twist and squeeze,
And I knew this was it.
He was just past me now
And I could see others up the trail.
I waited just a few seconds longer,
Then, I aimed and squeezed the trigger,
Like they had taught me
So long ago and far away.
He screamed and gurgled as he fell.
I got sick then and retched a while,
And then I was more alone.

MORTAR ATTACK
Written in Vietnam

I was lyin' on my bunk
Writing home that night.
The stars seemed to make peace
With the whole world.
This kinda put me in a soft mood,
An' made me feel deep down inside
That everything, everywhere was fine.

Then all hell broke loose on the east perimeter.
I got up to watch the tracers;
They were sure purty,
Goin' every which way,
An' making intricate patterns
Across the black night sky.
Then I heard this WHUMP............WHUMP,
An' wondered where it came from.

As I looked out the door,
Very strange an' slow-like
The NCO barracks erupted
And fell in slow motion.
I kinda squeezed up inside,
An' ran for my flack-jacket an' M-16.

Then all around me
The world seemed to go crazy.
It heaved an' roared at me,
An' I found myself getting up
From somewhere.

I was havin' some trouble
With my right leg, it was kinda numb,
I got purty mad then an' cursed some.

Next thing I knew
I was flyin' through the air
An' kinda hazy like
Wondered what had happened.

I could see what seemed to be
Just about everything flyin' through the air with me.
I thought it was sort of funny
Then the whole world hit me in the face.

ULTIMATELY

Written in Vietnam

This ignominious ball on which we dwell,
Still sings of war, of lust and hateful strife,
Still twists her tortured flesh, her soul to hell,
And plays the atoms threat to scorch our life.

Her despairing face is turned each smoldering day,
To gather in the life-light from out our sol,
That burning orb, which sends her living ray
To touch each man yet feed his greedy soul.

And yet a small pure pearl must still exist
On some forlorn, long-forgotten, shady place
Where angels tread and leave their gentle kiss,
Where raging storms have lost their mangling race,
Or man, his world and soul would long be dead,
His loving God and Angels would have fled.